IMAGES
of America

ST. GABRIEL'S
EPISCOPAL CHURCH

IMAGES
of America

St. Gabriel's
Episcopal Church

Judith Westlund Rosbe

ARCADIA
PUBLISHING

Published by Arcadia Publishing
Charleston, South Carolina

Library of Congress Control Number: 2020947718

For all general information, please contact Arcadia Publishing:
Telephone 843-853-2070
Fax 843-853-0044
E-mail sales@arcadiapublishing.com
For customer service and orders:
Toll-Free 1-888-313-2665

Visit us on the Internet at www.arcadiapublishing.com

*This book is dedicated to my husband, Robert L. Rosbe Jr.,
and to our two daughters, Kristina Westlund Rosbe, M.D.,
and Heather Rosbe Vrattos.*

CONTENTS

ACKNOWLEDGMENTS

All of the images in this book are from the archives of St. Gabriel's Episcopal Church at the Sippican Historical Society. A few years ago, the vestry of St. Gabriel's asked the Sippican Historical Society to take custody of the church's archives to protect them with climate-controlled storage and to enter the documents into the society's database so that they would be available for online research.

I especially want to thank Mallory Waterman, senior warden; Janet Bullock, parish administrator; Rev. Cathy Harper, deacon; and Rev. Robert Malm, interim rector of St. Gabriel's, for their assistance with this book. Leslie Thayer Piper, former music director at St. Gabriel's and now executive director and archivist of the Sippican Historical Society, also assisted me throughout and helped with research.

Many members of St. Gabriel's helped me identify persons in the photographs: Liz Brainard, Danielle Coffin, Alane Hall, Doug Harper, Rick Laine, Liz Leatham, Jane MacDonald, Hanna Milhench, Louise Nadler, Mary Pierce, Geoffrey Piper, Dave Sullivan, and Suzy Titus. Lyn Hovey provided me with information about his stained-glass company. I am also grateful to my husband, Bob Rosbe, who assisted me throughout this project.

—Judith Westlund Rosbe
Parish Historian,
St. Gabriel's Episcopal Church

Board of Directors,
Sippican Historical Society

INTRODUCTION

Located on the southeast coast of Massachusetts, the town of Marion is 60 miles south of Boston, 20 miles southwest of Plymouth—where the Pilgrims landed—and 11 miles east of New Bedford, once the whaling capital of America. A small town, Marion has only 5,100 year-round residents, but in the summer, its population grows to 6,080. It covers approximately 14 square miles with 25 miles of coastline.

Though Marion was originally inhabited by the Sippican Native Americans, a community of the Wampanoag tribe, Pilgrim families from Plymouth Plantation settled what is present-day Marion in 1678. The town was incorporated in 1852. Its residents chose the name Marion to honor a Revolutionary War hero from South Carolina, Francis Marion, whose guerrilla tactics were admired.

Thanks to its seaside location, Marion's economy centered on shipbuilding, whaling, fishing, and salt making. During the late 19th and early 20th centuries, Marion became popular as a summer resort where visitors enjoyed yachting, recreational fishing, and the town's beaches.

Rear Adm. Andrew A. Harwood wanted to live by the ocean during his retirement from the US Navy and chose Marion. He brought his family to vacation at the Bay View House hotel (before it grew to become the Sippican Hotel) in 1871. Several Episcopalians also staying in the hotel invited Admiral Harwood to conduct Sunday church services in the parlor of the hotel, because they knew he had been accustomed to conducting onboard church services in the Navy. The following summer, in 1872, Harwood purchased from the Sherman family a permanent home in Marion across the street from the Bay View House. (The Harwood home is presently owned by the Beverly Yacht Club for its clubhouse.) Harwood continued conducting Episcopal services in his home until 1874, when he purchased the Sippican Seminary school building at public auction for $700.

The Sippican Seminary had been built in 1847 as a private school for the daughters of sea captains. The land was purchased from Ronald and Polly Luce for $100, and 18 citizens of Marion put up the money as shareholders to build the school. In 1855, when enrollment dwindled, the Town of Marion rented the building, and it became Sippican Academy, a public school. The town rented the lower room for $12 per term and the upper room for $9 per term. In 1860, the upper room was also rented to the Sons of Temperance one evening a week for 20¢ per evening and to the Band of Hope (a temperance organization for children) every Saturday afternoon for 20¢ each meeting. Also in 1860, the three managing shareholders, Stephen D. Hadley, Henry M. Allen, and John Pitcher, granted the library association the right to use the second floor for a library at no cost. In 1874, the shareholders decided to sell the building at a public auction. Admiral Harwood stepped up to purchase the building, and it became the new home for Episcopal services in Marion.

The church was named St. Gabriel's Episcopal Church because of a promise Admiral Harwood made while battling a fierce storm at sea. He called upon the archangel Gabriel for deliverance from the storm and vowed to build a church in Gabriel's name if he survived. The small group of Episcopal summer worshippers formed a mission church, and by 1896, year-round services were offered. St. Gabriel's was consecrated on June 23, 1900, and shortly thereafter became an official church. Many distinguished clergy from the Episcopal Theological Seminary in Cambridge, Massachusetts, served the church in the early 1900s.

In 1913, St. Gabriel's was fortunate to hire America's most famous stained-glass artist, Charles J. Connick. His studio ultimately designed 11 memorial stained-glass windows for St. Gabriel's Chapel. The first, the Crocker memorial window, was dedicated on January 1, 1914, and installed behind the altar in the chapel. It was constructed with slab glass in the style of the medieval art form, but it also was designed in the modern American Arts and Crafts style.

The 1940s–1960s were marked by expansion of the congregation, acquisition of adjacent land, and building a parish hall, church school buildings, and a new sanctuary. Full-time rectors came to St. Gabriel's beginning in the 1950s. The first was Rev. John J. Albert (1951–1956), and the second was Rev. Donald D. Gardner (1956–1967). When Rev. Ernest W. Cockrell (1967–1992) arrived at St. Gabriel's, his first duty was the ground-breaking ceremony for the new sanctuary, which was consecrated in 1971. When Reverend Cockrell left after 25 years, Rev. Robert "Woody" W. Woodroofe III became the fourth rector (1994–2007) and was involved in major renovations in the sanctuary. The next rector was Rev. Geoffrey T. Piper (2008–2019), who was present during the time of additional capital projects including the courtyard and the addition of solar panels on the church roof.

The parish has been very fortunate to have welcomed assistant rectors and a deacon over the past three decades: Rev. Beulah C. Koulouris (1990–1993), Rev. Beth Maynard (1997–2000), Rev. Cynthia Bell (2001–2007), and Rev. Catherine Harper, deacon (2013–2020).

St. Gabriel's congregation today has around 300 families. The parish actively supports fellowship, lay eucharistic ministry, mission and outreach (local and global), music, newcomers, pastoral care, stewardship, and worship support. The parish opens its doors to the local community and beyond, celebrating Sunday services as well as weddings, baptisms, funerals, and memorial services, and openly welcomes other organizations such as Alcoholics Anonymous and Cub Scout Pack 32 to use its campus.

As St. Gabriel's prepares to celebrate its sesquicentennial in 2021, it continues to bear glad tidings, as did its namesake archangel.

One

EARLY HISTORY

St. Gabriel's Chapel was built in 1847 as a private school for the daughters of sea captains. The land was purchased for $100, and 18 citizens in Marion put up the money as shareholders to build Sippican Seminary, as the school was named. In 1855, when enrollment dwindled, the Town of Marion rented the building, and it became the public Sippican Academy. In 1874, the shareholders decided to sell the building at a public auction. Rear Adm. Andrew Harwood purchased the building for $700 to establish a church. He was born in 1802 and grew up in Bucks County, Pennsylvania, the son of John Edmund Harwood and Elizabeth Franklin Bache; he was a great-grandson of Benjamin Franklin. At the age of 16, he joined the Navy as a midshipman, and spent his entire career in the Navy before retiring in 1871. Because he wanted to live by the sea in his retirement, he brought his family to vacation at the Bay View House in Marion in 1871. Several Episcopalians also staying in the hotel invited Admiral Harwood to conduct Sunday services in the parlor. In 1872, Harwood purchased a home across the street from the Bay View House, and continued conducting Episcopal services in his house until 1874. The church was named St. Gabriel's because of a promise Harwood made while battling a storm at sea; he called upon the archangel Gabriel for deliverance and vowed to build a church in Gabriel's name.

In 1847, the land on the corner of Front and South Streets was purchased from Ronald and Polly Luce for $100, and 18 citizens put up the money to build Sippican Seminary. The school was later remodeled, and the top floor was removed when it was purchased to become St. Gabriel's Episcopal Church.

Sippican Seminary.

This early print of Sippican Seminary shows that the building originally had two floors. In 1860, the Town of Marion rented the upper room to the Sons of Temperance one evening a week for 20¢ and to the Band of Hope every Saturday afternoon, also for 20¢.

At right is a c. 1863 photograph of Rear Admiral Harwood. He retired to Marion in 1871 and began church services for Episcopalians in the summers, first at the Bay View House hotel and then at his newly purchased permanent home in Marion. The engraved portrait of Admiral Harwood below is from after the Civil War.

This is an engraving of the Bay View House, which was built in 1794 by the Hiller family on the corner of South Street and Harbor Lane (now Water Street). In 1882, the Sippican Hotel was added on the Harbor Lane side, and the Sippican Hotel Casino for dances and tennis was added across the street on the harbor.

In 1872, Rear Admiral Harwood purchased a house across the street from the Bay View House hotel from the Sherman family. He conducted Episcopal services in his home until 1874, when he purchased the Sippican Seminary building at public auction. The Harwood home is presently owned by the Beverly Yacht Club for its clubhouse.

Marion Plymouth Co Mass
November 7th 1874.

Received of A. A. Harwood. U.S.N. the
Sum of Three hundred and ten dollars and Seventy
nine cents in part payment of purchase of Sippican
Seminary and for back rent of the same

Henry M Allen
agent

$310.79

At the public auction of Sippican Seminary, Admiral Harwood was the highest bidder. This is the original receipt given to Harwood for $310.79 for partial payment for the purchase and for back rent. After payment in full, Harwood donated the building to begin St. Gabriel's Episcopal Church. He became authorized and licensed by the Episcopal bishop to conduct services as a lay reader in Marion.

EPISCOPAL CHAPEL AND FRONT STREET, Marion, Mass.

This is a c. 1890 postcard of St. Gabriel's Chapel after it was remodeled to remove the second floor of the Sippican Seminary.

EPISCOPAL CHURCH,
MARION

A fence was added a few years later, along with a bell tower, as shown on this postcard.

This interior view from 1890 shows a pot-bellied stove on the left, oil lamps, and a two-rank reed organ on the right. An eagle lectern was installed as a memorial to Admiral Harwood.

Admiral Harwood had a daughter, Elizabeth Franklin Harwood, who was called "Bessy." She was engaged to marry a young man who went off to fight in the Civil War. He died in the war, and Bessy remained single for the rest of her life. She was very active in the early church and was instrumental in inviting her childhood friend Richard Watson Gilder, the editor of *Century Magazine*, to vacation in Marion during the summers. He, in turn, invited many of his famous friends (including Pres. Grover Cleveland and his wife, Frances) to visit Marion in the summertime. President Cleveland loved to fish in Buzzards Bay, and his wife made many friends in Marion. In fact, they were so fond of the town they even named one of their daughters Marion. This photograph shows "Aunt Bessy" with two of the Gilders' children, Rosamond and George.

On September 22, 1875, Allen Harwood, aged eight, died of diphtheria at the home of his grandfather, Rear Adm. Andrew Harwood. The town authorities gave permission to bury the body in the chapel yard. A marble cross marks the spot. This is the only burial in the chapel yard, although ashes are now interred in the grass plot of the courtyard.

The Harwood family gravesite is in Old Landing Cemetery in Marion.

Two

EARLY MEMBERS

In 1898, Capt. Zenas Hinkley Crocker became the first warden of St. Gabriel's Church. He was born on August 25, 1845, in Wareham, Massachusetts, a son of Walton N. (a harness maker) and Elizabeth Swift Crocker. Educated in the public schools of Wareham, he went to sea on a merchant vessel at the age of 17. He gradually worked his way up to first mate and at the age of 27 was given command of a vessel. For 20 years thereafter, he sailed as master of various vessels. In some he was a part owner, and his ventures in general freighting and in foreign trade were very successful. In 1891, he retired from the sea, moved to Marion, and became the proprietor and manager of a lumber and coal yard. On January 6, 1896, Captain Crocker married Mary Hammatt Hathaway, the daughter of Capt. John K. Hathaway of Marion. He was 51 years old, and she was 33. Captain Crocker died of cancer in 1902 at the age of 56. In 1909, when Mary died, she left $4,000 to St. Gabriel's Church in her will for a memorial fund, part of which was used to purchase the Crocker memorial stained-glass window in the chapel. Julia DeWolf Gibbs, a summer resident of Marion and an accomplished artist, enhanced the interior of St. Gabriel's Chapel with several significant works of her art. In 1889, she married an Episcopal priest, Daniel Dulaney Addison, who regularly preached at St. Gabriel's Chapel. In 1884, Julia donated a beautiful stained-glass dove window made with her own hands as a memorial to her brother. It was she who suggested the Boston stained-glass artist Charles J. Connick, who made the magnificent Crocker memorial stained-glass window over the altar. In 1920, she painted a triptych of Saint Cecilia, the patron saint of music, with an angel on each side of her, in memory of her mother; it is located near the organ. In 1921, Julia embroidered and donated to the chapel a lovely green dossal that, in gold embroidery, quotes Luke 1:19: "I am Gabriel that stand in the presence of God and am sent to speak unto thee and to shew thee these glad tidings."

Capt. Zenas Hinkley Crocker was the first warden of St. Gabriel's Church. The success he had as a sea captain aided St. Gabriel's immensely when he and his wife died and left $4,000 to the church.

Church records show that in 1909, Mary Crocker's estate gave $4,000 to St. Gabriel's Church: $1,000 devoted to the support of preaching and $3,000 for memorial windows. At the suggestion of Julia DeWolf Gibbs Addison, the magnificent Crocker stained-glass window was made by renowned artist Charles J. Connick and installed over the altar in the chapel, where it remains today.

Both Zenas and Mary Crocker are buried in Old Landing Cemetery in Marion. They both died on January 21, seven years apart.

Julia DeWolf Gibbs Addison's mother was one of the founding members of St. Gabriel's. Julia was born in Boston in 1866 and was educated in England by a governess. She then returned to Boston, where she studied art. She was also the author of poems, plays, songs, and Christmas carols.

Julia DeWolf Gibbs Addison (right) plays Ophelia in an artistic production. She was a skilled craftswoman of ornamentation, mosaics, metal work, and embroideries.

Julia DeWolf Gibbs Addison wrote a memoir of her life in Marion in the 1880s. She recounts how she remembered the Gilders, who came to Marion at the invitation of a childhood friend, Bessy Harwood, the daughter of Rear Adm. Andrew Harwood, the founder of St. Gabriel's Church.

MARION IN THE EIGHTIES

By JULIA DE WOLF ADDISON

WHEN I undertake to write about Marion in the eighties, I wish it understood that I was young in those days, and knew nothing about politics, conditions, or any larger questions. Marion was my Summer home — in my "vacation days," and I can only give you what I knew personally of this most interesting period in the history of the Summer colony.

Of course the chief center was the studio, with the matchless Gilders dispensing their informal hospitality to the noted people who thronged to the place. I remember the first time Mr. and Mrs. Gilder came to see Marion, and the circumstances were as follows:

Miss Bessie Harwood, a daughter of Admiral Harwood, brilliant, talented — a writer of good stories and a clever actress — had made a great reputation as Mrs. Jarley, in animated wax-work shows which she organized. The Admiral was the son of an actor, who had married the granddaughter of Benjamin Franklin. Miss Bessie came honestly by her ability. During the Civil War, she had been a nurse in Washington hospitals, and had raised large sums of money in various places by giving Jarley Wax Work Shows.

In "The Critic," April 30, 1892, Joe Gilder published an appreciation of Miss Bessie Harwood's impersonation:

[1]

Julia DeWolf Gibbs Addison donated a beautiful stained-glass dove window made with her own hands as a memorial to her brother, Franklin Bradford Gibbs. It remained over the altar until it was moved forward in 1913 to make room for the magnificent Crocker memorial window behind the altar. She suggested to the memorial committee that they hire stained-glass artist Charles J. Connick, who had recently set up his workshop in Boston. It was the beginning of a long relationship between the Connick workshop and St. Gabriel's resulting in 11 stained-glass windows in the chapel today.

In 1920, Julia painted a triptych of Saint Cecilia, the patron saint of music, with two angels. It is located to the right of the organ in the chapel. She presented it in memory of her mother, who helped establish St. Gabriel's.

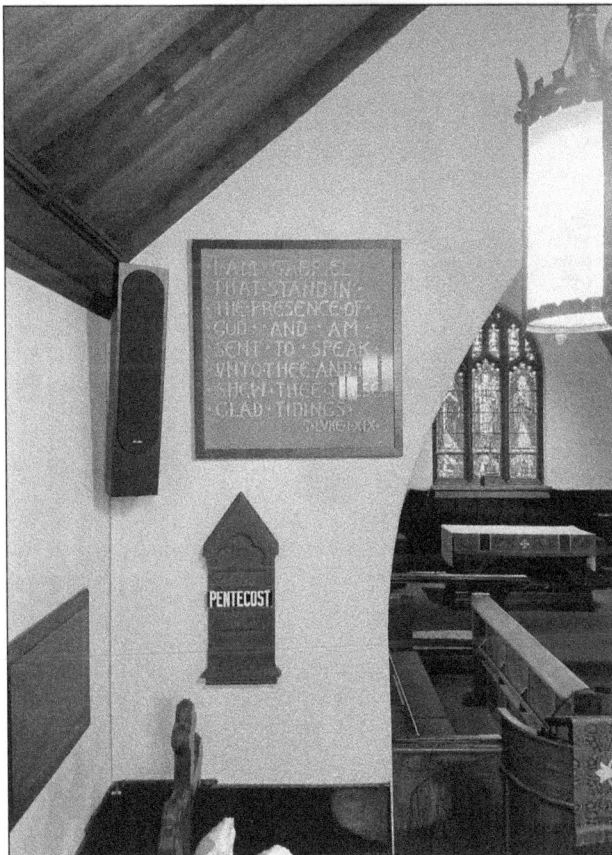

In 1921, Julia embroidered and donated to the chapel a lovely green dossal with gold embroidery that reads, "I am Gabriel that stand in the presence of God and am sent to speak unto thee and to shew thee these glad tidings." It is now framed and is on the left wall in front of the altar.

Clergyman Dies

Served Episcopal Church
50 Years; Burial Will
Be in Marion

Dr. Daniel D. Addison of Brookline and Marion, widely known Episcopal clergyman who had served the church 50 years, died in Brookline yesterday at the age of 73.

He was rector emeritus of All Saints Church in Brookline after serving that church as rector many years.

Funeral services will take place at the Brookline Church at 3:30 p. m. Monday with Bishops Lawrence, Babcock and Sherrill and Dean Milo Hudson Gates of the Cathedral of St. John the Divine, New York, officiating. Burial is to be in Marion where Dr. and Mrs. Addison summered for many years.

Spoke Here Frequently

Dr. Addison was known to many churchmen and Episcopalians here because of having spoken frequently at Grace Church and St. Martin's Church. He also spoke on many occasions in the town church at Marion and at community services.

Born in Wheeling, W. Va., March 11, 1863, a son of Thomas Grafton and Marie Elisson Addison, he was graduated 20 years later from Union College. He studied three years at the Episcopal Theological School at Cambridge where he received his doctor's degree.

From 1886 to 1889, he served as an assistant at Christ Church, Springfield and in 1889 married Julia DeWolf Gibbs, who survives him. For six years after leaving the Springfield church he was rector of St. Peter's Church in Beverly.

DR. DANIEL D. ADDISON

Dr. Addison was named rector of All Saints Church in Brookline in 1895, an assignment he held 26 years until 1930 when he became rector emeritus. He was a trustee of the Brookline Public Library, registrar of the Episcopal Diocese of Massachusetts, trustee of the College of Monrovia, Liberia, director of the Church Temperance Society, president of the Massachusetts Clerical Association and chairman of the trustees of the Donation for Education group in Liberia.

He was known for many of his written works including "Lucy Larcom: Life, Letters and Diary," "Life and Times of Edward Bass, First Bishop of Massachusetts," "The Clergy in American Life and Letters" and "The Episcopalians." He was a member of the London Authors' Club, Boston Authors' Club and Harvard Club.

Besides his widow, Dr. Addison leaves a daughter, Julia Dulany Addison. Mrs. Addison is known as a designer and an authority on ecclesiastical ornamentations. She also is author of several books.

Julia DeWolf Gibbs married Daniel D. Addison, an Episcopal rector. He preached often at St. Gabriel's when he and his wife spent summers in Marion. He gave the sermon in 1924 when St. Gabriel's celebrated its 50th anniversary.

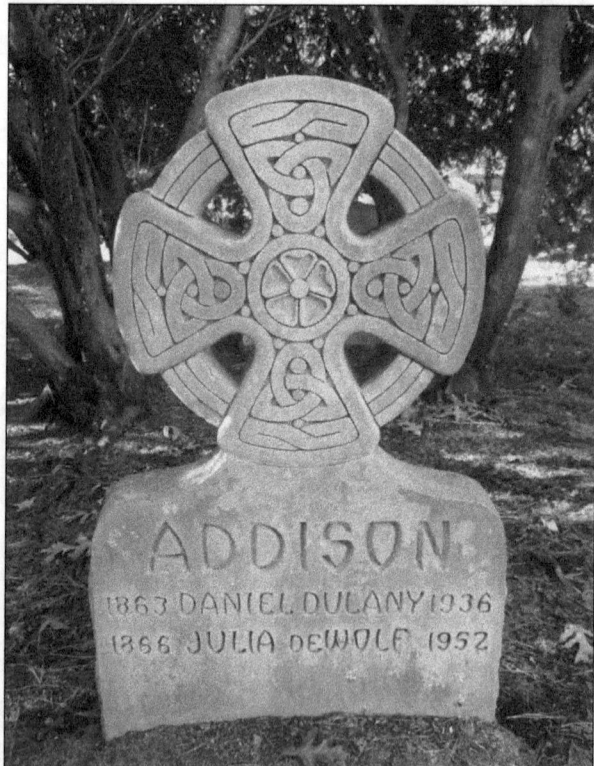

Both Daniel and Julia are buried in Marion's Evergreen Cemetery.

Three

FAMOUS WEDDING AND CONSECRATION OF CHAPEL

Marion's most prominent portrait painter, Cecil Clark Davis, and the most prominent journalist in the United States, Richard Harding Davis, were married in St. Gabriel's Chapel on May 4, 1899, to national fanfare. Both the Clark and Davis families were summer residents of Marion, which is how the couple met. Cecil was born in Chicago in 1877. Her father was a successful businessman and a partner with Alexander Graham Bell. He was also the collector for the Port of Chicago during the 1893 World's Columbian Exposition. The Clark family purchased a large, rambling 23-room cottage on 10 waterfront acres in Marion. The Davises, from Philadelphia, were their summer neighbors on Harbor Lane (now Water Street). Richard Harding Davis, the famous war reporter ("the white knight of journalism"), novelist, and playwright, attended dances at the casino across from the Sippican Hotel and noticed the beautiful Cecil Clark, whose mother played the piano for the dances. Richard was 35 years old and Cecil was 21. Their wedding at St. Gabriel's Chapel was an international event. Ethel Barrymore was maid of honor. Charles Dana Gibson, the famous illustrator of "Gibson Girls," was a groomsman, and Rev. Percy Browne officiated. Cecil and Richard traveled all over the world. They lived in London and Paris, and when Richard was assigned to cover the Boer War in Africa, Cecil went with him. Thus began the pattern of their life together, traveling wherever his assignments took him. After 13 years of marriage, they divorced, and Richard married 19-year-old Bessie McCoy, the "Yama Yama Girl," in 1912. After that, Cecil devoted herself to her painting and to her many dogs. She died at the age of 78 and is buried in Evergreen Cemetery in Marion. On June 23, 1900, one year after the famous marriage, St. Gabriel's Chapel was consecrated.

On May 4, 1899, Cecil Clark and Richard Harding Davis's wedding party enters St. Gabriel's Chapel before the ceremony. Journalists and photographers lined up outside the fence.

This photograph shows the decorated interior of St. Gabriel's Chapel before the wedding ceremony.

Cecil and Richard Harding Davis are pictured leaving the church after the wedding.

The wedding party poses in this photograph. The bride wore white lace over shimmering satin. The party included well-known figures such as Ethel Barrymore (the young woman on the left, next to Cecil) and Charles Dana Gibson (second row, second from right). Gibson used the likeness of Richard Harding Davis for the man who accompanied the Gibson Girl, who was similar to Cecil—beautiful, athletic, and independent.

Fred Barden's horses and carriage were used for the Cecil Clark and Richard Harding Davis wedding on May 4, 1899, at St. Gabriel's Chapel. Barden was dressed in formal attire, including a silk hat, as he drove the bridal surrey. He scrubbed the white Morgan horses until they were pink, and the harnesses were bedecked with white ribbons and bows so that the leather did not show. A part of the stone wall at the Clark residence had to be taken down to widen the drive to let the carriage through. This photograph was taken on South Street in front of Union Hall.

This portrait was taken at the reception at the Clark home on Harbor Lane. It is unusual in that actresses Ethel Barrymore and Sissy Loftus are at center. The bride is fifth from the right (next to her father-in-law in the wicker chair), the groom is seated in front of his father, and the two mothers are on the far right.

This is another photograph taken at the wedding reception at the Clark home.

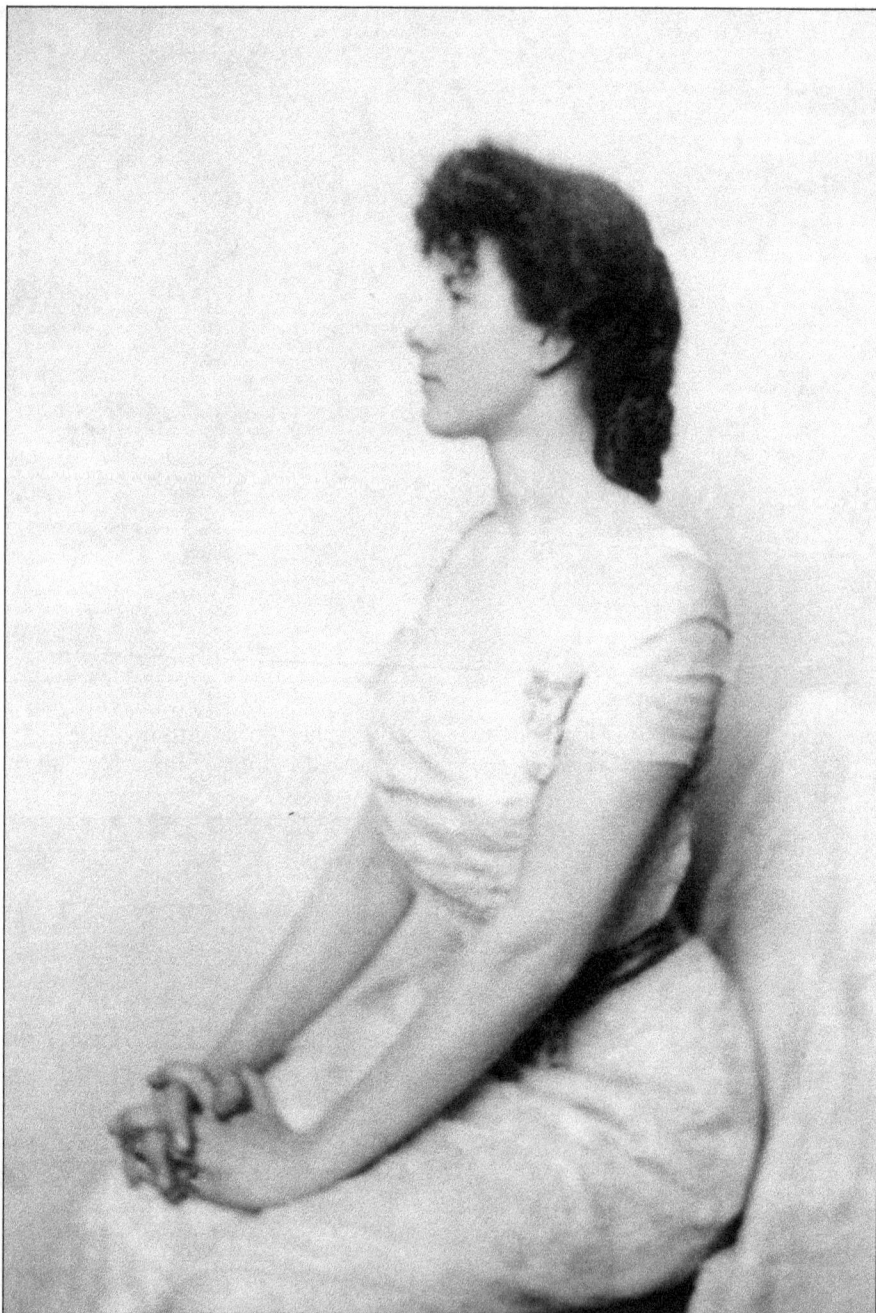

This is a photograph of Cecil Clark Davis, Marion's most famous painter. Over the course of her life (1877–1955), she developed into an award-wining portrait artist who painted many of the important people of her era, including Charles Lindbergh, actor Lionel Barrymore, Arctic explorer Roald Amundsen, and inventor Alexander Graham Bell. The daughter of a successful Chicago industrialist who summered in Marion, Davis was interested in painting, sports, games, music, theater, and dogs. In 1899, her wedding to renowned journalist, novelist, playwright, and war correspondent Richard Harding Davis was reported from Marion as a social event of national interest.

These two photographs show Cecil Clark Davis painting outdoors on Harbor Lane (now Water Street) in Marion overlooking the harbor. She was mainly a self-taught artist, but many sources state that she was taught by the renowned John Singer Sargent. Davis kept a diary most of her life, and according to an entry in 1908, she first met Sargent in London in December, noting that she found him a "simple forceful person." On January 3, 1909, her diary entry read, "John Sargent came in after luncheon very nervous and perhaps shy, but a vast volcanic man—took him to the studio which he loved—thought the monochrome painting unnecessary. Admitted that no one could teach anyone anything but the technical part—mechanics of the trade. He played the piano for me charmingly and asked me to tea on Wednesday."

Cecil Clark Davis receives a kiss from one of her large dogs. She owned 35 dogs, each a different breed.

This is a photograph of Richard Harding Davis in Marion, where he spent summers. He was often portrayed accompanying Gibson Girls by his friend artist Charles Dana Gibson.

This photograph of Richard Harding Davis was taken in the small house on Main Street that he rented as his office and is addressed to Charles Hellier of Marion.

This photograph of Richard Harding Davis was taken during the Spanish-American War. It is inscribed to Louise Clark, mother of Cecil Clark Davis and a good friend of Richard.

This is a watercolor painting of Richard Harding Davis painted by Cecil Clark Davis.

In 1899, Cecil Clark Davis married the renowned journalist novelist, playwright, and war correspondent. His assignments led the pair into a marriage of world travel, which gave Cecil access to a vast array of international art and artists. Later divorcing Richard, Cecil devoted the rest of her life to painting. This portrait of Richard Harding Davis was painted in 1906 and is in the collection of the Sippican Historical Society in Marion.

Cecil Clark Davis and Richard Harding Davis are pictured together at their home in Marion.

From left to right, Cecil Clark Davis, Ethel Barrymore, and Richard Harding Davis pose with bicycles in Marion. Ethel and Richard were childhood friends; in fact, she was the maid of honor in both of his weddings: first to Cecil and then to Bessie McCoy.

Cecil Clark Davis was buried in Evergreen Cemetery in Marion in 1955 at the age of 78.

ST. GABRIEL'S CONSECRATED.

Impressive Ceremony at Marion's Quaint Little Chapel.

Bishop Lawrence Assisted by Many Visiting Clergymen.

Place of Worship First Established Years Ago by Admiral Harwood.

In the presence of a large number of visiting clergymen, St. Gabriel's chapel at Marion was consecrated this morning by Right Rev. William Lawrence, D. D., bishop of the diocese of Massachusetts. The chapel has been used for services during the summer for a number of years, but as it was not until this year that it was freed from encumbrances, the consecration has of a necessity been delayed. The present minister in charge is Rev. John C. Brooks, rector of Christ church, Springfield.

In honor of the event the quaint little chapel was simply but prettily decorated with flowers. The chancel was filled with ferns, daisies and laurel, and the same were grouped effectively elsewhere in the chapel.

The bishop and the visiting clergymen were met at the entrance of the chapel by the executive committee, consisting of Edward S. Hamlin, E. Crocker and John M. Allen. They then marched up the aisle to the chancel, repeating the 24th Psalm, beginning "The earth is the Lord's," alternately, the bishop one verse, the clergy the next. After the bishop had taken his seat within the rails, the instrument of donation and endowment was read by the treasurer, Mr. Allen, declaring that the chapel was free from all lien or encumbrance. It was then presented to the bishop.

The regular prescribed form of service for the consecration of a church or chapel was read by the bishop. The sentence of consecration, in the bishop's name, was read by the minister in charge, Rev. John C. Brooks. Following the consecration service came morning prayer, conducted jointly by a number of the visiting clergymen. Then came the ante-communion service, with a sermon by Bishop Lawrence and the visiting clergymen by Edward S. Hamlin, a member of the executive committee, at his home on Front street.

Among the out of town clergymen present were Rev. Percy Brown, Rev. D. D. Addison, who were former ministers in charge at Marion; Rev. Augustus Prime of Brighton, and Rev. J. F. Kinsman, rector of St. Martin's, New Bedford. Invitations were sent to all the clergy of the archdeaconry of New Bedford.

The Episcopal form of service was first established in Marion about a quarter of a century ago by Admiral Harwood, U. S. N., a retired naval officer, who made the town his home. He himself, as lay reader, conducted services for many years in the upper room of the old Sippican seminary on South street. Later he bought the building, and changed it into the chapel which is the edifice consecrated today.

As time went on and Marion became more frequented as a summer resort, services were held by various clergymen. Among these were Rev. Dr. Leighton Parks of Boston, Rev. Percy Brown of Roxbury, Rev. F. W. Tompkins, Rev. D. D. Addison and Rev. Frederick Towers of Cambridge. Rev. Mr. Brooks took charge last summer.

It was in St. Gabriel's chapel that Richard Harding Davis and Miss Cecil Clark were married a year ag-

rence, the confirmation service, and the celebration of the holy communion, which marked the close of the ceremonies.

After the services at the chapel, a collation was tendered to Bishop Law-

ST. GABRIEL'S CHAPEL, MARION.

This is a newspaper article about the consecration of St. Gabriel's Chapel on June 23, 1900. The act of declaring the chapel sacred occurred once it was free of encumbrances.

Four

STAINED-GLASS WINDOWS BY CHARLES J. CONNICK

Charles J. Connick (1875–1945) was born in Springboro, Pennsylvania, into a family of modest means. When his father became disabled and unable to work, Connick left school in his teens to work as a newspaper illustrator for the *Pittsburgh Press*. Subsequently, stained-glass artist J. Horace Rudy recognized his talent and employed him as an apprentice in Rudy Brothers' stained-glass studio-workshop in Pittsburgh, where he was first introduced to the medieval glazing tradition. In 1908, Connick moved to Boston to work for another stained-glass studio, Spence, Bell & Co. He met MIT architecture professor Ralph Adams Cram in 1909 and began the most important professional relationship of his life. After a salary dispute with Spence, Bell & Co., Cram lent money to Connick to tour England and France and to study stained-glass windows, especially the English Arts and Crafts windows of Christopher Whall. Upon his return to Boston, and with the assistance of funds loaned by Cram, Connick opened a stained-glass studio of his own, Charles J. Connick Associates, at Nine Harcourt Street in Boston's Back Bay in 1912. When the Mary Crocker estate left $3,000 to St. Gabriel's for memorial windows, a summer parishioner, artist Julia Gibbs Addison, recommended that the memorial windows committee (Harriet Hamlin, Miss J. Wisner, Mrs. John M. Allen, Dan Kane, and Levi Wing) ask Connick to design a memorial stained-glass window. In 1914, the window was installed in the south wall of the chapel, where it majestically resides over the altar today. This was the first of 11 stained-glass windows that Connick and his studio designed for St. Gabriel's Chapel. After Connick's death, his craftsmen continued to operate the studio until 1986, when it finally closed.

Charles J. Connick was the greatest American stained-glass artist of the 20th century.

This photograph shows an artist-craftsman at work in Charles J. Connick's Harcourt Street studio in Boston around 1915.

Charles J. Connick and his colleagues view one of their stained-glass windows in the studio at Harcourt Street in Boston.

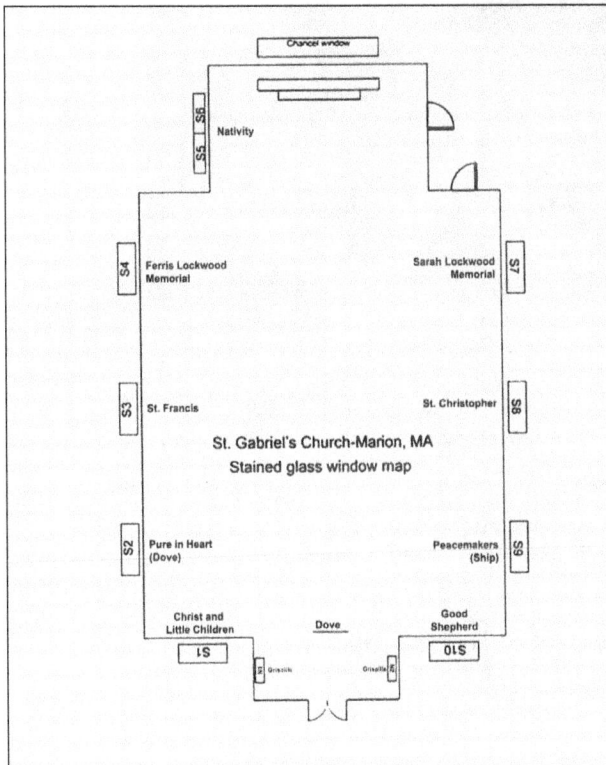

Chancel window

S5 | S6

Nativity

S4 — Ferris Lockwood Memorial

S7 — Sarah Lockwood Memorial

S3 — St. Francis

S8 — St. Christopher

St. Gabriel's Church-Marion, MA
Stained glass window map

S2 — Pure in Heart (Dove)

S9 — Peacemakers (Ship)

Christ and Little Children

Dove

Good Shepherd

S1

S10

Griselda

Griselda

This is a window map of the stained-glass windows in St. Gabriel's Chapel.

The Crocker Memorial Window, located over the altar of St. Gabriel's Chapel, was dedicated on January 1, 1914. It was given in memory of Capt. Zenas Hinkley Crocker; his wife, Mary Hammett Crocker; and his mother, Elizabeth Swift Crocker. The stained-glass window was constructed with slab glass in the style of the medieval artform but designed in the modern American Arts & Crafts style. The window is made up of lancets (large middle panels), predella (square panels at the base), and tracery (small panels at the top). The main lancets in the center, from left to right, depict the Virgin Mary, Saint Gabriel the Archangel, and Saint Elizabeth. The predella panels, from left to right, depict the Annunciation to the Virgin, Zacharias and Gabriel, and Gabriel with Daniel, a Hebrew priest. In the tracery are four kneeling angels holding (from left to right) a pot with three lilies, an inn in Jerusalem where Jesus was born, a pelican piercing her breast to feed her young, and a lamb lying down on a dais. Below the predella panels from left to right are the inscriptions "Mary Hammett Crocker/Zenas Hinkley Crocker/and Elizabeth Swift Crocker." Charles J. Connick also signed his name in the lower right border of the right predella with the date. The frame was designed by a young man who had grown up in Marion, Edwin C. Luce Jr., who worked in the architectural office of Shepley, Coolidge & Rutan in Boston. Charles A. Coolidge donated his services as architect of the enlarged chancel.

This stained-glass window was given in memory of Sarah Wisner Lockwood (1850–1944). It was made in 1947 in a grisaille pattern with an anchor in the top medallion. The work order states that the window was to be designed as a companion to the harmonies and complement the earlier one with the same general character but with interesting variations.

This stained-glass window was given in memory of Mary Ballantine Cumming (1870–1934). It shows Saint Christopher in a fur gown with a red robe wading barefooted with the infant Jesus on his shoulder. Jesus holds an orb with a cross on the top. It is signed "Connick Associates" in the lower right corner. The work order stated that the date of completion of the window was spring 1955 and that this window would balance the opposite one devoted to Saint Francis.

This window was made in memory of George Stevenson Morse (1860–1932) and Estella Hughes Morse (1865–1937) in 1955. It states: "Blessed are the peacemakers for they shall be called the children of God." The work order stated that the window was to be "designed in the geometric and foliated pattern to harmonize with the others, and the traditional symbol of the Barque of Peter with sail inscribed with the Cross, dominates the upper portion."

This stained-glass window was made in memory of Alphonse William Query Sr. and Oris Hayden Query in 1961. It shows Christ as the Good Shepherd holding a lamb and surrounded by sheep, with an image of St. Gabriel's Church at upper right. The work order stated that the date of completion was Easter, April 2, 1961. It also stated that the window was based on one that was admired in Concord, Massachusetts.

This window was made in 1963 in memory of Millar Brainard (1895–1953), the first senior warden when St. Gabriel's officially became a parish. It depicts a seated Christ surrounded by children with nautical symbols. The work order gave very specific instructions: "The Child in Christ's arms should be looking up at Him—the others not looking directly at Him, except the one standing beside him holding a flower up toward Him and looking at Him. All the children to be kept in light garments, their faces to be pleasant, and lovely. . . . Keep plenty of rich blue in the backgrounds. Field is enriched with the growing tree and rose patterned border, and is in harmony with the present balancing window. Small symbols through the field suggest the sea—the sailboat and fish. Shells will also be included." The order emphatically stated that the halo was not to "look like a life preserver." The cross with a gavel and keys at upper right is the senior warden's insignia.

This stained-glass widow was made in 1953 in memory of Beryl Keith Kane and is inscribed "Blessed are the pure in heart for they shall see God" and "To the glory of God and in loving memory of Beryl Keith Kane 1865–1952." The work order called for "foliated pattern and colorful interlacing strap work supporting the dominant symbol of the Descending Dove of the Holy Spirit. . . . The anchor of Hope is introduced as a secondary symbol below, and the border is enriched with the lily of Purity."

This window was made in 1953 in memory of Russell Henry Leonard (1888–1949). It depicts the standing figure of Saint Francis in a brown robe with bare feet surrounded by birds and flowers. It is signed "Connick Associates" at lower right. The work order stated that Saint Francis was to be depicted "in a brown robe, not as broken in color as the one in St. George's, Roseburg, without the violet. Mrs. Leonard likes the face of the Roseburg, Saint Francis."

This stained-glass window was made in 1931 in memory of I. Ferris Lockwood (1855–1927). It is made in a grisaille pattern with a Greek cross bottony.

This window was made in memory of Edward and Katharine Brooke Hamlin and Harriet G. and Jane G.C. Hamlin. It depicts the Virgin Mary and Jesus. She faces left, with a blue robe over a white mantle, and kneels with her hands folded. He is swaddled from waist to feet and lies in a manger. There is an angel in the peak.

Five

RECTORS AND
ASSISTANT RECTORS

According to the Episcopal denomination, a new church is called a mission church, which means that it is under the direct guidance of and partially supported by the diocese. In the beginning, the bishop authorized and licensed Rear Admiral Harwood to conduct the services of the new mission church as a lay reader. His license was renewed and kept active until he died in 1884. The early church met only in the summer, because most of its members were summer residents. In 1875, services were held from May 23 until November 1. During the year, extensive alterations and improvements were made to the chapel. Visiting vicars (priests in charge of a supported mission), appointed by the bishop conducted services at the early church. Rev. John Cotton Brooks, a summer resident in Marion who officiated for many years in the summer, was paid $15 per Sunday. His home was at the northwest corner of Water and Allen Streets. Two other summer residents, Rev. Percy Browne of Roxbury and Rev. Daniel Dulaney Addison of Cambridge, also conducted services in the summer. In 1886, a stove was installed, and church services began to be held year-round. On July 6, 1904, cash on hand was $14.81. The mission church grew throughout the years, and in 1952, the diocese approved St. Gabriel's application to become a parish. Not only does a parish designation mean that the church is self-supporting, it also means that the church has a greater degree of independence in how it operates and chooses its own rectors. It also sends money to the diocese to support other mission churches. Today, the church has 300 families on its rolls.

In 1881, Rev. Percy Browne built a summer home in Marion designed by the famous architect Henry Hobson Richardson. He preached at St. Gabriel's and was the minister who officiated at the marriage of Cecil Clark and Richard Harding Davis in the chapel in 1899.

This photograph of Reverend Browne's newly constructed summer home was taken in 1881, right after it was built. It was the smallest home designed by Henry Hobson Richardson and cost $2,500.

REAR OF PERCY BROWNE'S HOUSE, MARION.

This is a rear view of Reverend Browne's home drawn by Mariana Griswold Van Rensselaer. She wrote the first definitive biography of her friend Henry Hobson Richardson two years after his death. *Henry Hobson Richardson and His Works* remains the foundation of all scholarship about Richardson and is the authoritative biography of the architect.

This c. 1900 photograph shows Rev. John Cotton Brooks, the first resident summer vicar at St. Gabriel's.

This drawing of Reverend Brooks's cottage in Marion, which was built in the spring and summer of 1882, was done by the architect John M. Allen.

This photograph, taken in 1885, shows Reverend Brooks, his wife, and two daughters on their porch in Marion facing Harbor Lane (Water Street).

This photograph of the home of Reverend Brooks was taken in 1898 from the Allen Street side.

At the suggestion of the bishop, Rev. Alfred Reed Hill of Staatsburg, New York, served as rector of St. Gabriel's from 1928 to 1930. His salary was $2,500 per year with a rectory at the corner of Main and School Streets (leased by the church), and a car. During his first year in Marion, he also taught English at Tabor Academy.

In 1931, the bishop appointed Rev. Dr. Charles Lincoln Taylor, a professor of the Old Testament at the Episcopal Theological School in Cambridge, Massachusetts, as the church's minister-in-charge. He remained for 13 years, until 1944. He did not live in Marion and ultimately left to become the dean of the Episcopal Theological School. In 1938, he facilitated the organization of St. Gabriel's Altar Guild, and in 1940, the parish hall was built.

From 1944 to 1946, another professor at the Episcopal Theological School, Rev. Richard S.M. Emrich, served as rector of St. Gabriel's. He left to become suffragan bishop of Michigan.

The bishop selected another professor from the Episcopal Theological School, Rev. Dr. Charles H. Buck Jr., as rector of St. Gabriel's. He served from 1946 to 1949.

From 1951 to 1956, Rev. John J. Albert of Troy, Ohio, was resident rector of St. Gabriel's. The church built a rectory on the corner of Converse Road and Allen Street for him and his family, and finally, St. Gabriel's had a full-time resident rector again. He assisted the church to apply for parish status, which occurred on March 16, 1952. St. Gabriel's was now a self-supporting parish with a greater degree of independence.

Reverend Albert assisted the young adults at St. Gabriel's to form a group called the Hornblowers to put on plays as a fundraiser for the church. One of the plays Reverend Albert directed was *You Can't Take It With You*. From left to right are (first row) Katheryn Babbitt, Marilyn Heikoff, Frantz Warner, and Minna Andres; (second row) Al Query, Peter Freedman, Sue Roche, Ted Babbitt Jr., Hilliard Lubin, Rev. Lawrence Somers, James Babbitt, Audrey Goodwin, Brooks Hawkins, Mary Betty Albert, Robert Snyder, Dr. Ray Baxter, Warren Ide, Alys Nowell, and Dr. James Arne.

Another successful play put on by the Hornblowers was *My Three Angels*, a comedy written by Samuel Spewack and Bella Spewack set in the penal colony on Cayenne, French Guiana, in 1910. The three angels are actually convicts who assist the family that owns the general store. This photograph shows, from left to right, (first row) director Rev. John Albert and Rick Angle; (second row) Don Durfee, Dick Peters, Hilly Lubin, and Ellie Freedman; (third row) Clayton Livingston, Alys Nowell, Sue Roche, Ted Babbitt Jr., Winthrop Baylies, and Jack Somers.

Another production of the Hornblowers was the stage farce *See How They Run*, by the British playwright Philip King. This popular comedy was written in 1945 about the comings and goings of clerics in an English vicarage during World War II, one of whom was an escaped Nazi prisoner-of-war in disguise. The cast, from left to right, included Ted Babbitt Jr., Peggy Dyer, Winthrop Baylies, Don Durfee, John Albert, Alys Nowell, Moa Andres, Hilly Lubin, and Franz Warner.

When Reverend Albert left to become the rector of All Saints' Church in Wynnewood, Pennsylvania, Rev. Donald D. Gardner became rector of St. Gabriel's from 1956 to 1967. He was raised in New Jersey, educated at Columbia and Hamilton, and graduated from the Episcopal Theological School in Cambridge.

This is a photograph of the Gardner family. From left to right are Betsy, Sue, and Don. They subsequently had two more daughters.

Reverend Gardner continued putting on plays with the Hornblowers as fundraisers for the church. In 1960, he acted as the character Judge Omar Gaffney in *Harvey*, which was directed by Ann Eaton.

◆◆

HARVEY

by Mary Chase

By special Permission of Dramatist Play Service, Inc.

Directed by Ann Eaton

CAST

(in order of appearance)

Myrtle Mae Simmons	Susan Roche
Veta Louise Simmons	Geraldine Schoeffel
Elwood P Dowd	Edwin V Babbitt, Jr
Mrs. Ethel Chauvenet	Peg Dyer
Ruth Kelley, R. N	Katheryn Babbitt
Duane Wilson	Dr Davis Gallison
Lyman Sanderson, M. D.	William Bradford
William R. Chumley, M. D.	Dr David MacFarlane
Betty Chumley	Marjorie Dyer
Judge Omar Gaffney	Rev Donald Gardner
C. J Lofgren	Robert Talbot

Rev. Ernest W. Cockrell was rector from 1967 to 1992, St. Gabriel's longest-serving rector. He graduated from Oklahoma City University and Harvard Divinity School. He completed a year of Anglican studies at the Episcopal Theological School and was ordained in 1965. He came to St. Gabriel's at the age of 28 and was the youngest rector in the history of the church. His first duty involved the groundbreaking ceremony for the new sanctuary, which was consecrated in 1971. He stated: "I came here during national turmoil over integration and Vietnam; ecclesiastical turmoil over social involvement and new liturgies; and local turmoil over the addition of a new sanctuary complex, and my Biblical liberalism."

This photograph was taken in 1992, before Jill and Ernest Cockrell left St. Gabriel's for California. There were many changes in society beginning in the 1960s, and Reverend Cockrell made many contemporary changes, such as folk masses, harbor services, and productions of *Godspell* and *Jesus Christ, Superstar*. The new church sanctuary was consecrated in 1971, which was 100 years after the church's founding.

Rev. Robert "Woody" W. Woodroofe III served as rector from 1994 to 2007. He graduated from Yale University and the Episcopal Theological School. While rector, he was involved with major renovations in the main church. During his tenure, St. Gabriel's became part of the Stephen Ministry, a program of lay-led pastoral care. He began the Journey to Adulthood program for teenagers, the Rite 13 confirmation program, and Godly Play classes for young children. He also started the Alpha Program, a 10-week program to introduce people to Christianity.

Rev. Geoffrey Tindall Piper served as rector from 2008 to 2019. He graduated from Amherst College and Bishop's University in Lennoxville, Quebec. During his tenure, the church entered into additional capital projects, including the church courtyard and the addition of solar panels on the church roof. As part of the church's mission program, the youth ministry group made service trips, each lasting one week, to Montana, Pennsylvania, West Virginia, Puerto Rico, and El Salvador. Reverend Piper's wife, Leslie, was the church's music director—she played the organ and directed the choir. She also started the South Coast Children's Chorus.

Rev. Beulah C. Koulouris served as assistant rector from 1990 to 1993. She was later an interim rector while the church searched for a new rector. A native of Plymouth, North Carolina, she was ordained in 1989. She attended Lynchburg College in Lynchburg, Virginia, Indiana University, and Columbia University, from which she received a master's degree. She received her master's of divinity from the Episcopal Divinity School in Cambridge. Formerly, Reverend Koulouris was active in lay ministry as an organist and choir director.

Rev. Beth Maynard served as assistant rector from 1997 to 2000. She graduated from Amherst College and received a master's of divinity from Boston University School of Theology, which included substantial coursework at the Episcopal Divinity School in Cambridge. She also received a certificate of advanced theological study from Seabury-Western Theological Seminary in Evanston, Illinois.

Rev. Mary Cynthia Bell served as assistant rector from 2001 to 2007. She graduated from Endicott Junior College, the College of New Rochelle, and the General Theological Seminary in New York City. She worked for many years at Doubleday Publishing Company before becoming ordained.

Six

EXPANSION AND
BUILDING PROJECTS

Over the years, the congregation grew and needed more space, so in 1940, a new parish house was added to the rear of the chapel. The architect was Henry R. Shepley, and the cost was $7,500. In 1951, the building next door to the church's property on South Street, Union Hall, was purchased to provide more room for the church school. The Hornblowers volunteered to repair and renovate the building. In 1954, the remainder of the upper room of the chapel was removed. In 1956, St. Gabriel's purchased the Santos property adjacent on Front Street for $15,000 for further expansion for a church school, day kindergarten, rector's study, and office. In 1957, the church had both Union Hall and the Santos home demolished, and in 1967, the church decided to build a new sanctuary and a new parish house and to remodel the existing parish house to provide a choir robing room, library, secretary's and rector's offices, and toilet facilities, with the present church remaining as is for use as a chapel. Stanmar Inc. of Sudbury, Massachusetts, prepared detailed plans and specifications and was hired to build the new facility, which was finished in the spring of 1968. The first service was held in the new sanctuary on Easter Sunday, April 14, 1968.

This photograph shows St. Gabriel's Chapel around 1920.

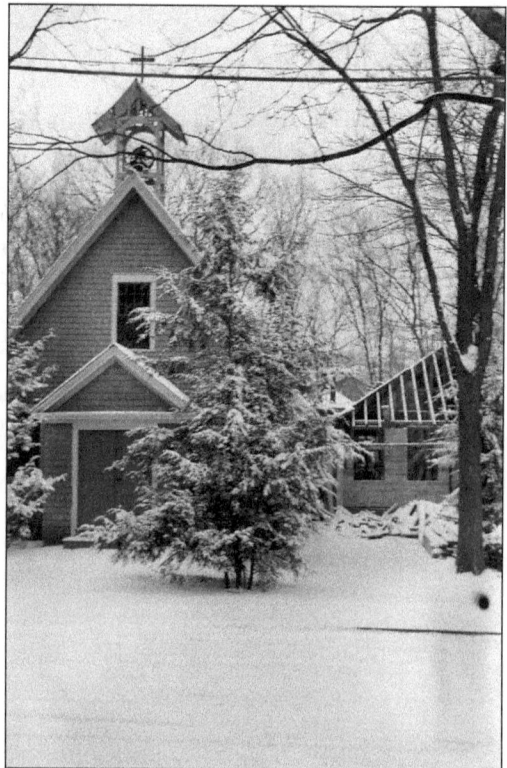

As the membership grew, the congregation decided that St. Gabriel's needed a new parish house and in 1935 began fundraising for it. This photograph shows the parish house being built.

These photographs were taken in 1940 as the new parish house was being added to the rear of the chapel.

Here are more photographs of the new parish house being built in 1940.

These photographs also document the new parish house being built in 1940.

This photograph shows the finished parish house from South Street in 1940.

This is a view of the finished parish house at the rear of the chapel from Front Street.

The dedication of the new parish house occurred on March 17, 1940. From left to right are Mable Jewett, Mary Rogers, Clara Wetmore, Jessie Perry, Martha Mayo, Harriet Cobb, Emily Wing, Elizabeth Richardson, Rev. Raymond Heron (suffragan bishop of Massachusetts), June Converse, Emma Angier, Dr. Charles Taylor, Donald Hood, Hilda Perry, Ann Wing, Ellen Richardson, Seth Cobb, Parker Converse, and Fred Wing.

Union Hall was built and paid for by Elizabeth Taber so that the women of the Congregational church in Marion would have a place to sew for their mission work. She purchased a lot on South Street on April 14, 1875, for $80, had a meetinghouse built, and gave the building, which she called Union Hall, to the Congregational Church Sewing Society. The building was adjacent to St. Gabriel's property.

Because Elizabeth Taber gave Union Hall to the Congregational church by her will, the church needed the permission of the Plymouth County Probate Court to sell the property. The church told the court that it did not have the funds to repair the building and would use the proceeds of the sale to repair the church basement. Once permission was granted, Dr. James Arne, a member of St. Gabriel's Episcopal Church, purchased the building on January 29, 1952, and immediately sold it to St. Gabriel's. The young adults in the Hornblowers group at St. Gabriel's volunteered their time to fix up the building so it could be used for a Sunday and nursery school and day kindergarten.

As the congregation grew, St. Gabriel's voted to raze Union Hall and to build a new church school building. It also purchased the adjacent Santos property on Front Street to square the boundaries. In 1957, the church conducted a successful campaign and raised $100,000 for the new church school building.

Members of the canvas committee for the church school building fund drive successfully raised the necessary funds. The committee members include, from left to right, (first row) Harold Nye, Rev. Donald Gardner, Russell Makepeace, Davis Taylor, and Frantz Warner; (second row) Donal Durfee, George Nowell, and Robert Talbot.

Ground Breaking Slated Tomorrow at Marion

Special to The Standard-Times

MARION, June 15—Ground-breaking ceremonies will be held at 10:15 a. m. tomorrow for the new St. Gabriel's Church school building.

Present for the ceremony will be the Rev. Donald D. Gardner, rector of the church, who will turn the first spade of soil. Also present will be the Vestry, Senior Warden W. Davis Taylor, Junior Warden Richard Angle and interested members of the church.

The work on the construction of the new building will start Monday. The contractor is J. J. Bumpus of Carver. Plans were drawn by architect George W. W. Brewster of Boston.

To date the amount of money collected or pledged is over $91,000 for a new building to be constructed on the ground that was occupied until last week by Union Hall.

On June 16, 1957, Rev. Donald D. Gardner turned over the first spade of soil for the new church school building.

This photograph shows the new church school building, which was completed in 1957.

Here are two more photographs of the completed complex showing the chapel, parish hall, and new church school building in 1957.

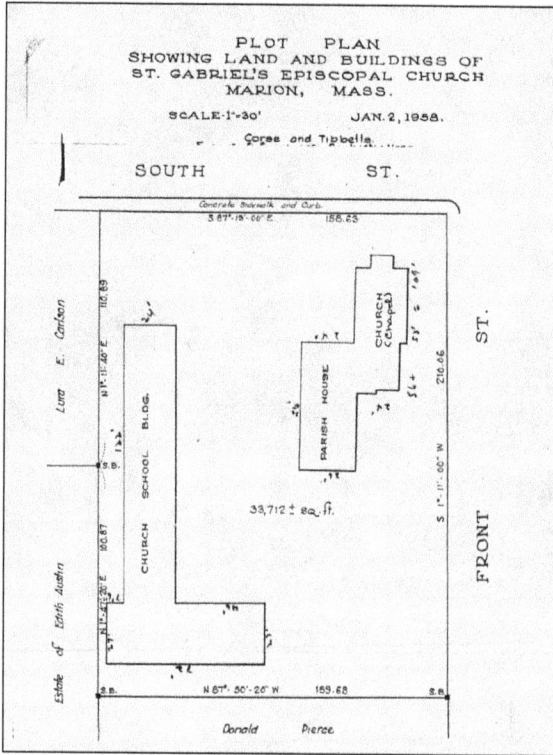

This plot plan by Corse and Tibbetts, dated January 2, 1958, shows the original chapel, the parish house, and the new church school building.

Church membership increased yearly, and the congregation decided once again in 1966 to fundraise in order to build a new parish hall and a new, larger sanctuary and to remodel the current parish house to provide a choir robing room, library, secretary's and rector's offices, and toilet facilities. The church employed Stanmar Inc. of Sudbury to prepare detailed plans and specifications to add the new church and parish hall. The chapel would remain as it was. Here is a drawing of the proposed new plan for St. Gabriel's, which would ultimately cost $175,000.

Russell Makepeace, the treasurer of St. Gabriel's in 1967, dutifully recorded in photographs the progress of the building of the new church and parish hall and the remodeling of the old parish hall. The photograph above shows the last view of the old church yard at 8:00 a.m. on May 20, 1967. Soon after, the heavy machinery appeared.

This photograph, taken on May 23, 1967, shows the site where the new church would be built. Note the huge boulders dug out from the ground.

On June 11, 1967, work began on the site of the new parish hall.

On July 6 and 7, 1967, prefabricated arches were installed for the new church.

St. Gabriel's Church
Building Program
Financial Status.
July 31, 1967

	ORIG. BUDGET	TO DATE COMMITTED	ESTIMATE TO COMP.	TOTAL EST. COST
GENERAL CONSTRUCTION	143,000	144,200	2000	146,200
MISCELANEOUS	—	1500	2000	3500
KITCHEN	2,000	—	2000	2000
FURNISHINGS	11,000	—	8500	8500
ORGAN	6000	10500	—	10500
LANDSCAPING	1500	100	1400	1500
INTEREST, ETC	5000	—	2800	2800
	168,500	156,300	18,700	175,000

This spreadsheet done by Russell Makepeace shows that the cost of the new building program had increased to $175,000.

This photograph was taken on July 18, 1967, and shows the progress on the new church.

This photograph records further progress on the new church building on July 21, 1967.

Russell Makepeace took this photograph on July 28, 1967, showing the large window opening in the new church, which eventually became a beautiful stained-glass window made by Lyn Hovey Studios.

On August 9, 1967, Russell Makepeace took this photograph of the renovations to the old parish house.

By August 19, 1967, the siding on the new parish house was installed.

The interior of the new parish house is pictured on September 28, 1967.

This photograph was taken on December 30, 1967, of the interior of the new church, which was set up for the first wedding to take place there, despite the fact that it was not finished yet. Rev. Ernest Cockrell had promised Audrey Goodwin in September that the sanctuary would be ready by Christmas so that her daughter could be married there.

Pamela Goodwin of Marion married David Binks of Australia in the new, unfinished church on December 30, 1967. There were no pews yet, an old kitchen table was used for an altar, and the festival frontal was borrowed from the Church of the Good Shepherd in Wareham to fit over the table. A white runner down the center aisle obscured the concrete floor, and chairs were brought in.

This is the announcement of their wedding. As it turned out, one of the wedding guests, Charles H. Jones, asked another guest why there were no pews. Upon learning that the church did not have any yet, he informed the rector that he had just purchased an old church in Whitman to use as a storage area for his shoe factory and that the church was filled with curved pews, which he offered free to St. Gabriel's. The only charge was $50 to have the pews delivered.

Pamela Goodwin
Bay State Bride
Of David Binks

1967

Special to The New York Times

MARION, Mass., Dec. 30 — Miss Pamela Jane Goodwin, daughter of Mr. and Mrs. Ernest Leslie Goodwin, was married here this afternoon to David Nisbet Binks, son of Mr. and Mrs. Norman Frederick Binks of Brighton, South Australia.

The Rev. Ernest W. Cockrell performed the ceremony in St. Gabriel's Episcopal Church.

The bride was given in marriage by her father, who is president of the Cape Cod Shipbuilding Company. She wore an ivory satin gown with kimono sleeves and yoke of English net trimmed with appliqués of re-embroidered alençon lace and seed pearls. Her bouffant tulle veil was attached to a matching lace headband, and she carried anemones and white heather.

Mrs. Paul Douglas Prevost was matron of honor. Bridesmaids were the Misses Joanne Asherman, cousin of the bride; Joanne Viecides and Sandra Wells. Louise Lalli was the flower girl. Gordon Leslie Goodwin, brother of the bride, served as best man.

Mrs. Binks was graduated from the Oak Grove School in Vassalboro, Me., Connecticut College and the Katharine Gibbs School in Boston.

Her husband, a graduate of St. Peter's College in Adelaide, Australia, is a builder of one-design sailboats. Last year he received a Churchill fellowship from the Australian Government to study boatbuilding abroad. His father, who is retired, was a civil engineer with the South Australian Engineering and Water Supply Department.

Howards
Mrs. David Nisbet Binks, was Pamela Goodwin.

The first service in the new
sanctuary occurred on Easter
Sunday, April 14, 1968. This
photograph was taken by
Russell Makepeace on May 3,
1968, from the balcony and
shows the finished interior
of the new church. The new
curved pews fit beautifully.

This aerial photograph shows
the completed St. Gabriel's
complex. The original chapel
is on the left, the renovated
old parish house is behind it,
and the new church is behind
the renovated parish house.
On the right is the new
parish house with the church
school building behind it.

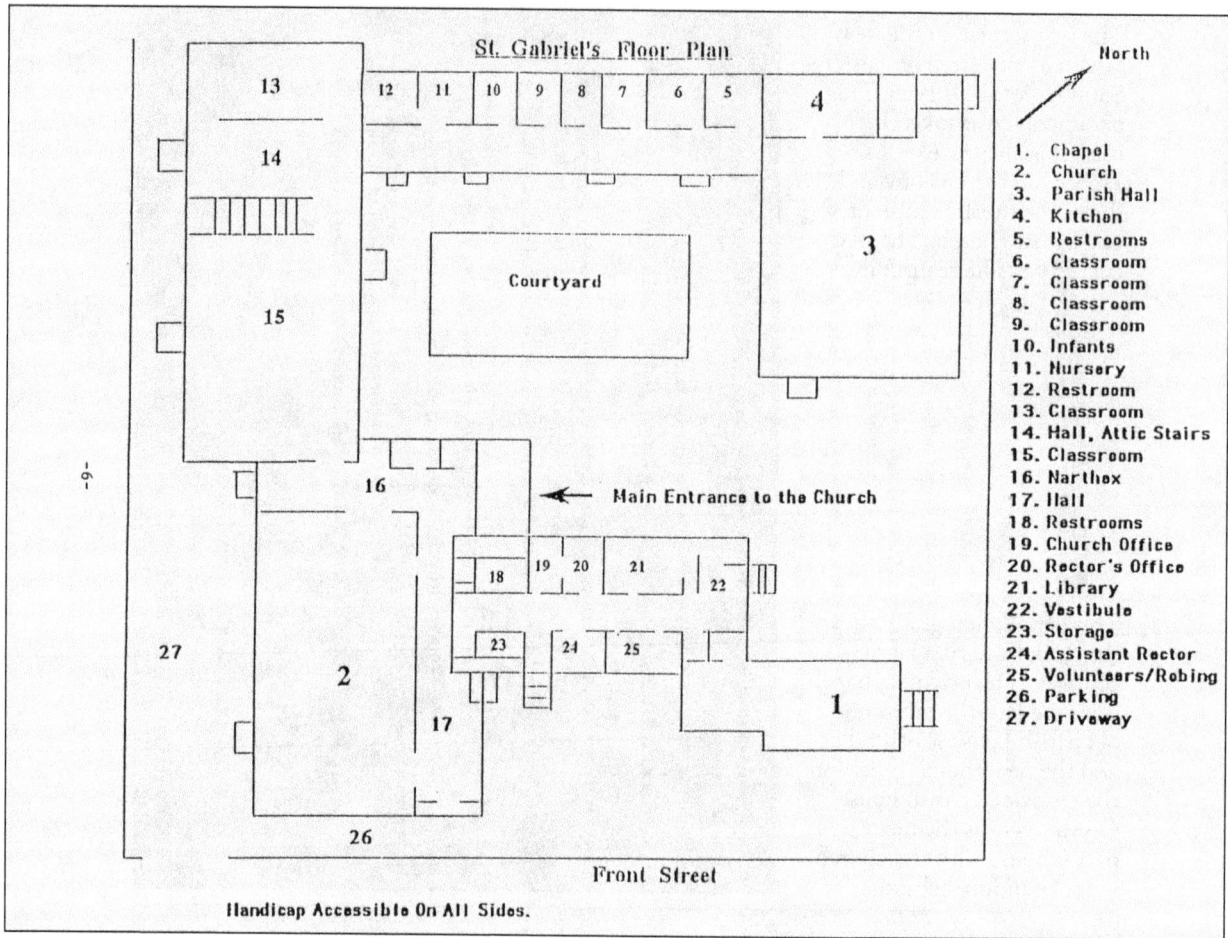

St. Gabriel's Floor Plan

North

1. Chapel
2. Church
3. Parish Hall
4. Kitchen
5. Restrooms
6. Classroom
7. Classroom
8. Classroom
9. Classroom
10. Infants
11. Nursery
12. Restroom
13. Classroom
14. Hall, Attic Stairs
15. Classroom
16. Narthex
17. Hall
18. Restrooms
19. Church Office
20. Rector's Office
21. Library
22. Vestibule
23. Storage
24. Assistant Rector
25. Volunteers/Robing
26. Parking
27. Driveway

Courtyard

Main Entrance to the Church

Front Street

Handicap Accessible On All Sides.

This is the floor plan of St. Gabriel's church today.

Seven

STAINED-GLASS WINDOWS BY LYN HOVEY STUDIO

Lyn Hovey is the president and artistic director of the internationally recognized Lyn Hovey Studio in Boston and Studio de Lyn Hovey in Guatemala. His distinguished career spans more than 50 years as an artist, teacher, lecturer, author, and leader in the stained-glass industry. He studied at the Cleveland Institute of Art and subsequently was accepted as an apprentice with a specialty in stained-glass painting at the Sandon Stained Glass Studio in Bratenahl, Ohio, a suburb of Cleveland. Two years later, in 1965, he was hired as a junior stained-glass painter and designer in the Boston studio of William Herbert Burnham, and later worked for Joseph G. Reynolds. Burnham and Reynolds are two of the more celebrated leaders of the Boston neo-Gothic stained-glass movement. In 1971, Hovey established his own studio in Cambridge, and in 2012 he moved his studio to Dorchester, Massachusetts. In 2003, he founded a branch studio in Antigua, Guatemala. Hovey has taught art throughout New England and in a variety of venues, from university art programs to inner-city after-school enrichment programs. In addition, he has authored many articles on stained glass. He was chosen by St. Gabriel's to make six stained-glass windows for its church. Three of his windows have been installed, two are currently being made, and one is in the design stage. The large window over the altar (*Gabriel*) was financed with fundraising by the parish. The second window (*Baptism*) was given by the Harper family, the parish, and Lyn Hovey. The remaining four stained-glass windows have been paid for by private donors who are members of the church. When the Charles J. Connick Studio closed, Hovey was able to purchase a substantial amount of stained glass that had originally been made in England from the studio.

These photographs show Lyn Hovey working in his stained-glass studio in Boston.

These images show workers in Lyn Hovey's stained-glass studio in Guatemala. Hovey is third from left above.

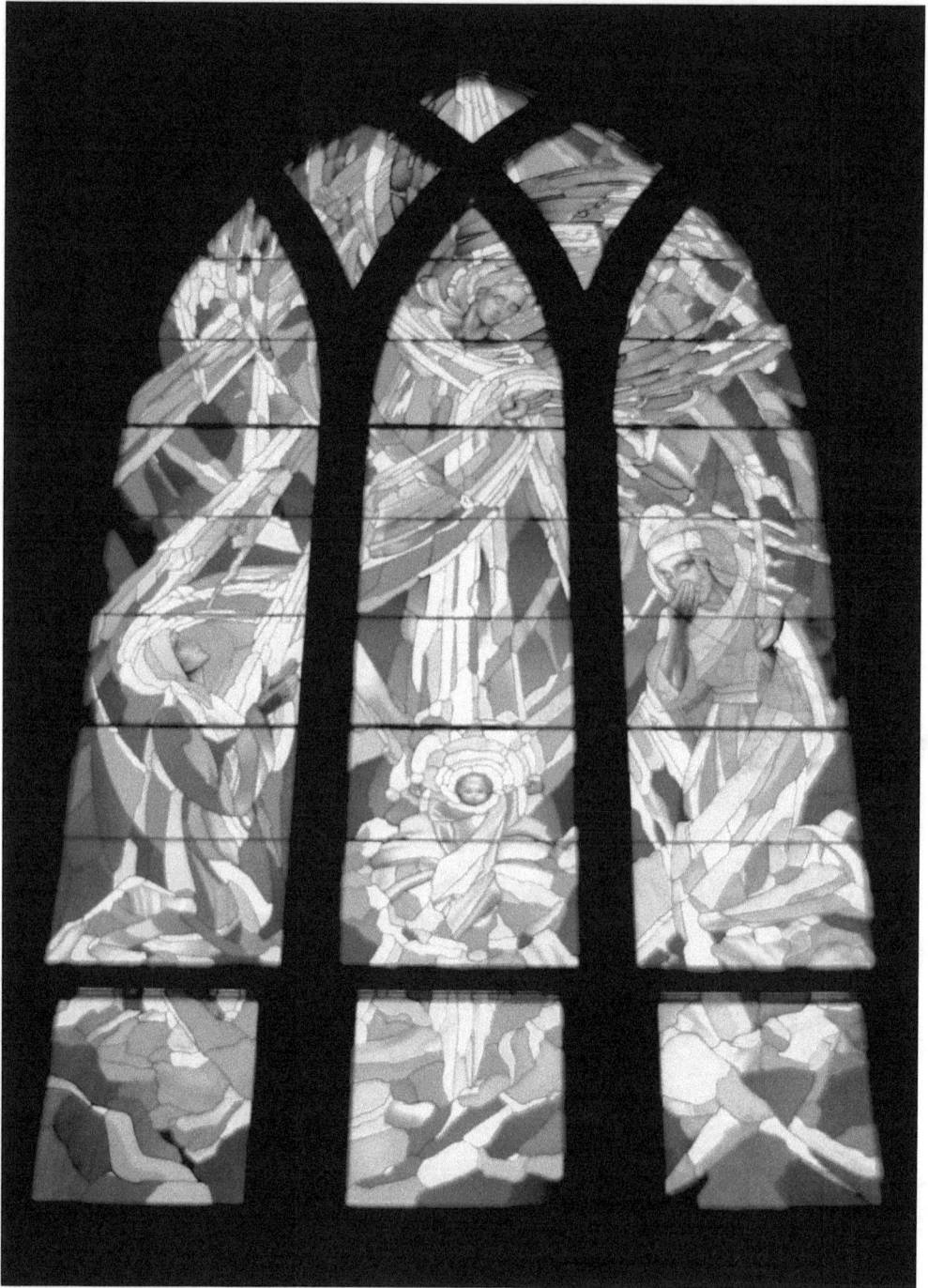

This is the first stained-glass window in the church designed by Lyn Hovey and made in his studio. Installed in 2006, it is called the *Gabriel* window and shows three appearances of Gabriel to Mary (left), to Zechariah (right), and to the birth of Jesus (center). Gabriel appeared to Mary and told her that she would give birth to a son, that she would name him Jesus, and that he would be the son of God. Gabriel also appeared to Zechariah and announced to him that his wife would give birth to a son, whom he was to name John, and that this son would be John the Baptist.

The second stained-glass window, the *Baptism* window, was given by the Harper family, the parish, and Lyn Hovey to celebrate Rev. Catherine A. Harper, the deacon at St. Gabriel's. The window depicts John the Baptist baptizing Jesus.

This photograph shows Rev. Cathy Harper at the celebration of the installation of the *Baptism* window in 2018. From left to right are Rev. Geoffrey Piper, Deacon Cathy Harper, Rev. John McGinn, and Lyn Hovey, the stained-glass artist who designed the window. Hovey also donated a substantial portion of his time in making the window.

The celebration included Reverend Harper's family. From left to right are granddaughter Caitlin Harper, husband Doug Harper, granddaughter Molly Harper, son Douglas Harper Jr., Deacon Cathy Harper, and Lyn Hovey.

This is the plaque beside the *Baptism* window.

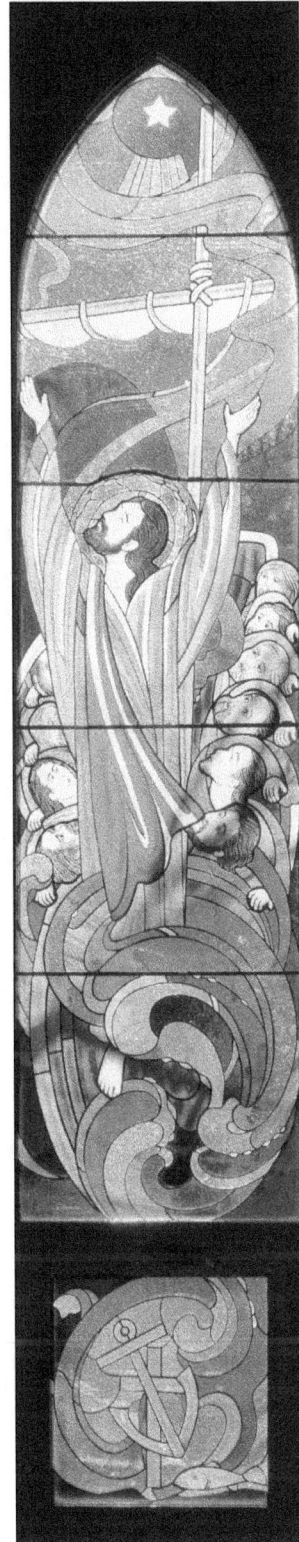

Another stained-glass window, *The Calming of the Storm*, was given by Jane H. Lonsdale in loving memory of her deceased husband, Capt. Adrian L. Lonsdale, who spent his career in the US Coast Guard. The plaque beside the window reads, "Even the winds and the sea obey him. Matthew 8:27. Given to the glory of God in thanksgiving for the blessings of faith, family, and friends."

Two other windows have been designed by Lyn Hovey and are now being assembled in his Guatemala studio. The See family has donated this window in honor of their deceased mother, Posy. They have chosen the verse "consider the lilies of the field, how they grow; they toil not, neither do they spin," from Matthew 6, as the theme. This is a watercolor painting of the window by Lyn Hovey.

This is a watercolor painting of another stained-glass window being assembled in Guatemala given by Judith and Robert L. Rosbe Jr. in celebration of their two daughters, Dr. Kristina Westlund Rosbe and Heather Rosbe Vrattos. It depicts the Resurrection in Matthew 28, when Mary Magdalene and the other Mary go to see the tomb, find it empty, and are told by an angel that Jesus has risen and gone to Galilee.

Eight

WOMEN OF ST. GABRIEL'S EPISCOPAL CHURCH

Since the beginning of St. Gabriel's Episcopal Church in 1871, women have played a vital role. In its early days, when St. Gabriel's was a mission church, the women headed up the church school and helped with fundraisers. They also played an active role in steering the direction of the early church. Early women members included Miss Wisner, Miss Horner, Mrs. Edward Hamlin, Margaret French, Sarah W. Harwood, E.H. Wisner, Miss Tappen, Mrs. John M. Allen, Mrs. Abbot, and Mrs. George Richards. In 1918, Mrs. Daniel H. Kane and Mrs. F.C. DeVeau ran the church school. According to records, the children raised $15 and gave $5 each to three missions. In 1928, St. Gabriel's established a branch of the Women's Auxiliary with 27 active members. This group was active until 1958, when it became the Women's Guild, which started as a sewing group for missions and branched out into church suppers and the summer fair. The Women's Guild was headed by Fran Arne, Sarah Gibbs, and Daisy Lovell. From the beginning, the chapel's altar was cared for by Sarah Harwood. When she became elderly, a formal altar guild committee was established that rotated women to set up the altars for Sunday worship services. The women of the church ran Fair Noel, a fundraiser in December before Christmas. It contributed substantially to church projects and mission work. From 2003 to 2016, the women ran a fundraiser in the summertime called Gardens-by-the-Sea that made almost $100,000 for the church. The women handbell ringers, headed by Sylvia Strand, provide music at church services.

This photograph shows the Altar Guild in 1973. Committee members include, from left to right, (first row) Edie LaGreze, Lillian Bete, Maisie Dawson, Helen Hellier, June Maxwell, and Peggy Dyer; (second row) Marion Hartshorn, Suzy Titus, Cindy Harlow, and Jill Cockrell.

This newspaper photograph shows the Family Fair in 1971. Committee members include, from left to right, Sarah Gibbs, Mary Tomlinson, and Eunice Eaton.

In 1968, (from left to right) Betsy Duncan, Eunice Eaton, and Liz Brainard show objects that they made to sell at the Fair Noel Christmas fundraiser.

This 1975 photograph shows Charlotte Richards and refurbished dolls to be sent to an Inuit mission in Alaska.

Suzy Titus (left) and Sylvia Strand sell flowers and wreaths at the Fair Noel Christmas fundraiser in 1976.

Sylvia Strand (left) and Margot (Arms) Stone were cochairs of the Fair Noel fundraiser in 1981.

From left to right, Mary Lalli, Joey Hetzek, and Gwennie Alexander have fun in the kitchen at the 1989 Fair Noel fundraiser.

Ellie Warner (left) and Liz Brainard arrange holly branches at the 1994 Fair Noel fundraiser.

Fair Noel was so popular in the community that long lines waited to get into the fair before it opened.

Shirlee Thomas (left) and Mary Wardle run the raffle table at the 1994 fair.

Betty Hooper replenishes the dessert table at the 1994 fair.

This table displays Christmas decorations made by the women of St. Gabriel's at the 1994 fair.

Sisters Lauren (left) and Elke Milhench help to make sandwiches at the 1994 fair.

From left to right, Joyce West, Dana Anderson, Ellen Stone, Louise Nadler, and Andrea Keene enjoy selling baked goods at Fair Noel.

From left to right, Suzy Titus, Sally Woodroofe, and Faith Paulsen enjoy working at Fair Noel.

The women handbell ringers provide music in 1994.

This is the invitation to the successful fundraiser by the women of St. Gabriel's. Gardens-by-the-Sea provided almost $100,000 for the church's projects and mission work.

Gardens by the Sea

A tour of private gardens sponsored by St. Gabriel's Episcopal Church Marion, MA

❂

Friday, July 25
10 am - 4 pm
&
Saturday, July 26
1 pm - 4 pm

Tickets:
$12 in advance
$15 day of tour

❂

Nine

CHURCH SCHOOL AND YOUTH ACTIVITIES

Since its conception, St. Gabriel's has considered the religious education of its children a top priority. Nursery school children participated in godly play activities. As the children got older, they learned Bible stories, studied the Bible, and participated in the choir. They also gave ecumenical folk concerts, put on the Christmas pageants, became acolytes, and did mission work in their community, other parts of the country, and abroad.

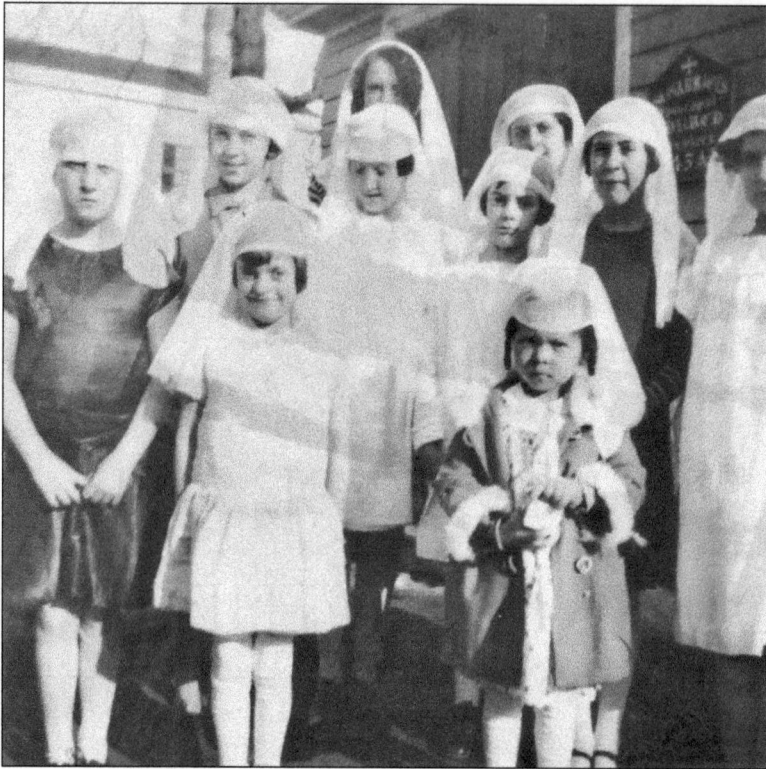

This photograph, taken in 1929, shows a girls' Sunday school class in front of St. Gabriel's Chapel.

The boys' choir is pictured in front of the chapel in 1929.

This photograph, taken in the early 1950s, shows a Sunday school class on its way to Boston. From left to right are (first row) John Parker, Freddie Campbell, and Richard Carson; (second row) Daisy Lovell, Polly Cotter, Sue Query, June Parker, Constance Whittaker, Rowena Love, Ruth Campbell, and C. Thomas Carson.

These photographs show church school in 1957.

Here are more photographs of children attending church school in 1957.

These photographs show children at church school in 1957.

This photograph shows the choir lining up and getting ready to sing in 1958.

Bill Blasdale, an acolyte, is ready to lead the choir into the chapel in 1958.

Here is another photograph taken in 1956 of the choir ready to enter the chapel. Rev. John Albert (far right) and Ted Babbitt Jr., a lay reader, are at the rear.

Rhone Blasdale (left) lines up with Bill Blasdale and Albert Ford before entering the chapel in 1956.

This photograph was taken in 1970 of the children's choir. From left to right are (first row) Matthew Keener, Randolph "Biff" Duncan, Kim Ann Eaton, Seth Nichols, and Bill Thomas; (second row) Hillary Thomas, unidentified, Michelle Nichols, and Debbie Nichols; (third row) Mark Hartshorn, unidentified, Elizabeth "BZ" Duncan, Elizabeth "Whippsy" May, and Kevin Eaton.

Rector Ernest Cockrell started this ecumenical youth folk rock group, called Guitar Masses, in the late 1960s. From left to right are Brenda Clarke, Debra Clarke, John Heuston, Teddy McCarthy, Karen Hayward, and Kim Barry.

In 1994, the youth group gets ready for a Christmas pageant. Some of the participants included Will Jeffrey, Sam Moore, Alex Duane, and Phoebe Stone.

These three camels performed in the 1994 Christmas pageant.

This photograph shows the three wise men in the 1994 Christmas pageant: from left to right, Devon Gaudet, Jeffrey Laine, and Andrew McGaffey.

The angels in the 1994 Christmas pageant are, from left to right, Augusta Nadler, Barbara Hall, Laura Duane, Courtney Birkins, and Audrey Blanchette.

This photograph shows the 1996 Confirmation class, led by Danielle Coffin. From left to right are (first row) Andrew Pendergast, Robbie Cowell, Matthew Kotowski, Connor Gaudet, Eric Pierce, Jeffrey Laine, and Charlie Coffin; (second row) Bonnie Kilpatrick, Caitlyn Babbitt, Courtney

Birkins, Audrey Blanchette, Lauren Marx, Barbara Hall, Andrea Caron, Molly Gilmore, Leah Latham, and Danielle Coffin.

From left to right, Acolytes Abigail Coffin, Hillary Prouty, and Elizabeth Coffin get ready for church in 1994.

Hillary Prouty (left) and Abigail Coffin lead in the choir in 1994.

These photographs show the youth mission group at work in Northfork, West Virginia, in 2018. They spent a week helping a community with painting and other chores. From left to right above are (first row) Phil Daniels, Kari Marvel, Georgia Toland, and Michael Bienz; (second row) Aila McEnroe, Laura Toland, Paige Feeney, Rev. Cathy Harper, and Rev. Geoffrey Piper. At left is the man whose house they were painting, and at right is the Mustard Seeds & Mountains advisor. Below are, from left to right, (kneeling) Aila McEnroe; (first row) Deacon Cathy Harper, Bess Marie Pierre, Kari Marvel, Georgia Toland, Isabelle Kelly, Paige Feeney, and Phil Daniels; (second row) Tyler Kelly, Marcus Pierre, Michael Kelly, Elke Pierre, Laura Toland, and Michael Bienz.

Acolytes are pictured with Deacon Cathy Harper in 2020. From left to right are (first row) Ivy Elger, Caroline Achilles, Lulu Johnson, Peter le Gassick, Gabriel Coughlin, and Sibley Casi; (second row) Tres Elger, Clara Bonney, Liza Feeney, Philip le Gassick, Deacon Harper, Anne le Gassick, Ella Milhench, and Darin Procopio.

Ten

OTHER CHURCH ACTIVITIES

Throughout the years, St. Gabriel's Episcopal Church has incorporated many activities to involve various members of its congregation. Because the town of Marion is on Buzzards Bay, many activities revolve around the ocean. In 1932, the church sponsored water sports and races as a benefit to make money. There is an annual blessing of the animals, today mainly cats and dogs, which the members bring to church once a year. In the summer, services have been held at Silvershell Beach, on boats in the harbor, and also at a local golf club. There is an active adult choir, men's fellowship, and friendship tables in which church members cook and serve dinner in St. Gabriel's Parish Hall to people in the greater community twice a month.

_1932_

Water Sports and Races

NYE'S PIER, MARION
Friday, August 19
BENEFIT ST. GABRIEL'S CHURCH

10 A. M.—OWNERS' RACES FOR 15-FOOTERS, 12-FOOTERS AND ROOKIES' FLEET, BOAT TREASURE HUNT.

11 A. M.—WATER SPORTS.

12 M.   —HOT DOGS, ICE CREAM AND MUSIC. EVERYBODY MUST BRING A BOX LUNCH AND THERMOS BOTTLE. BEAUTY CONTEST, GRABS, CAKE TABLE. AFTER LUNCH—OBSTACLE RACES, SPEED BOAT RIDES, FORTUNE TELLER, GAMES, EVENTS OF ALL KINDS.

SKIPPER'S RACE

THE BIG DAY OF THE SUMMER ON MARION HARBOR

A small entry charge will be made for each events, payable to the treasurer, H. Nelson Emmons, on the day of the sports.
IN CASE OF RAIN, FOLLOWING MONDAY

COURIER PRINT, WAREHAM

This 1932 brochure announces water sports and races on Marion harbor as a benefit for the church.

This photograph shows a harbor church service in the late 1960s. Rev. Ernest Cockrell presided, and a small keyboard provided music.

Rev. John Albert blesses the animals in 1954.

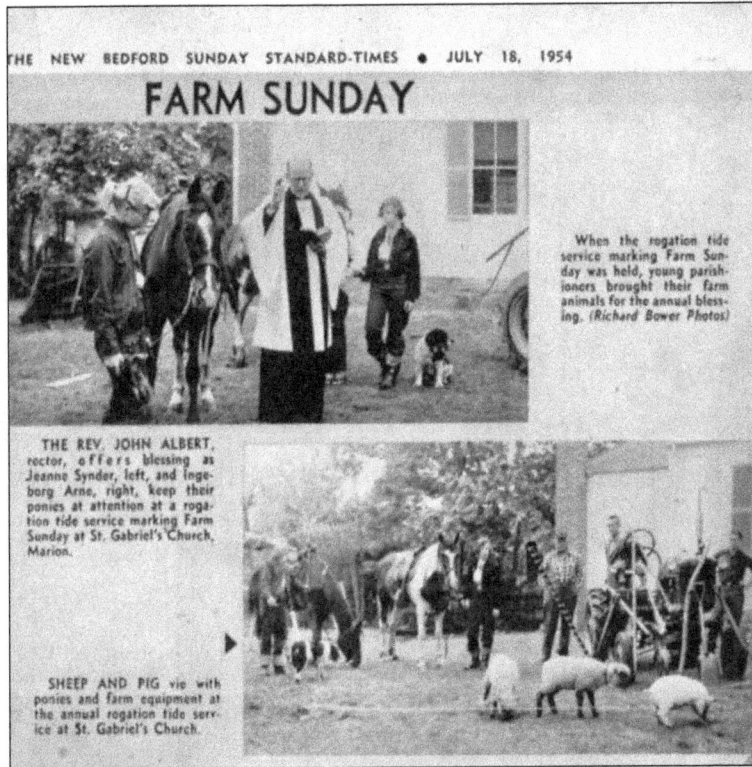

THE NEW BEDFORD SUNDAY STANDARD-TIMES ● JULY 18, 1954

FARM SUNDAY

When the rogation tide service marking Farm Sunday was held, young parishioners brought their farm animals for the annual blessing. (Richard Bower Photos)

THE REV. JOHN ALBERT, rector, offers blessing as Jeanne Synder, left, and Ingeborg Arne, right, keep their ponies at attention at a rogation tide service marking Farm Sunday at St. Gabriel's Church, Marion.

SHEEP AND PIG vie with ponies and farm equipment at the annual rogation tide service at St. Gabriel's Church.

Rev. Geoffrey Piper blesses Judie Kleven's dog in 2015.

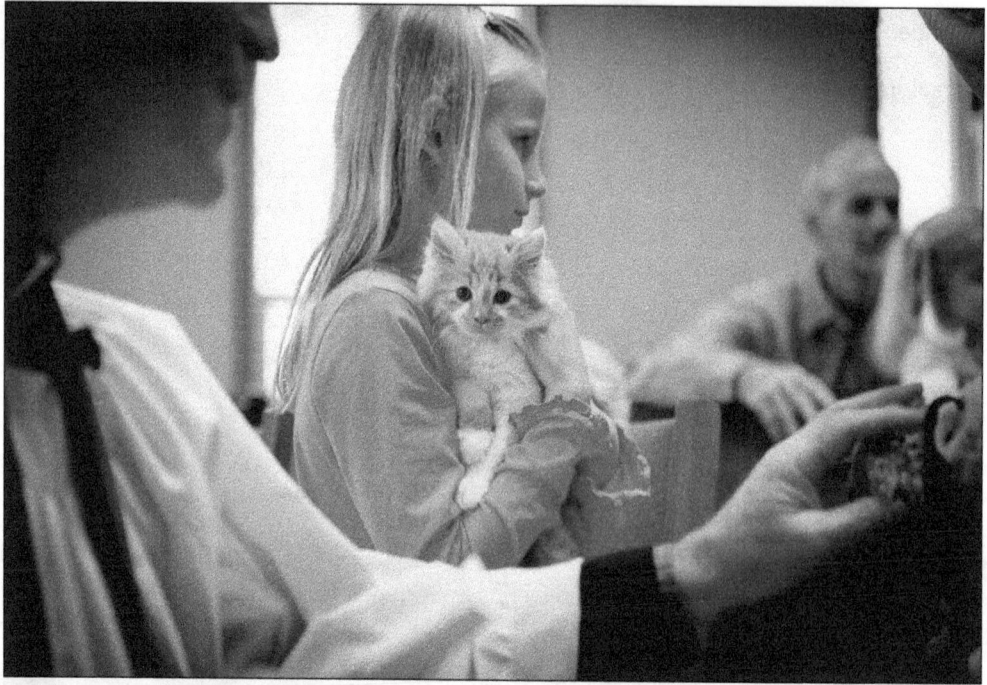

This young
girl's cat waits
to be blessed.

A bird is
being blessed
by Rev.
Geoffrey Piper.

Many weddings occur at St. Gabriel's. Here are Corinne and Jim Marlow with Reverend Cockrell after their wedding on October 19, 1988.

The choir has always been an integral part of the church service at St. Gabriel's. This 1994 photograph shows (from left to right) Ann Schenk, Suzy Titus, Elaine Caron, Joey Hetzek, Barbara Dadagian, Joan Roller, Pat Petit, and Faith Paulsen.

Men's Fellowship has also been an active organization in the church. Here Dick Anderson (left) presents an annual fellowship service award to Dick Swoish.

St. Gabriel's cooks and serves dinner in its parish hall to people in the greater community twice a month. Hanna Milhench has headed this activity for many years. Pictured from left to right are Bruce Breamer, Hanna Milhench, Marge Procopio, Patsy Easterly, Shirlee Thomas, Carol Dildine, and Bill Bixby.

These photographs were taken at the St. Gabriel's benefit Gardens-by-the-Sea.

This photograph shows another beautiful garden by the sea.

Truman Terrell accompanies the attendees at the Gardens-by-the-Sea benefit luncheon.

Visit us at
arcadiapublishing.com